101 Simple Things To Grow Your Business

by Dottie Walters and Lilly Walters

CRISP PUBLICATIONS, INC.
Menlo Park, California

101 Simple Things
To Grow Your Business

by Dottie Walters and Lilly Walters

CREDITS
Managing Editor: **Kathleen Barcos**
Editor: **Colleen Wilder**
Typesetting: **ExecuStaff**
Cover Design: **ExecuStaff**
Artwork: **Lilly Walters**

Copyright © 1996 by Crisp Publications, Inc.

Crisp Publications distributes world-wide.

Library of Congress Catalog Card Number 94-68300
Walters, Dottie and Lilly
101 Simple Ideas to Improve Your Business
ISBN 1-56052-316-6

About the Authors

Dottie Walters, has been the President of the Walters International Speakers Bureau for over 25 years. The editor and publisher of SHARING IDEAS newsmagazine, she is the author of numerous articles and books. A consultant for both businesses and speakers bureaus, Dottie has been interviewed on television and radio programs around the world.

Lilly Walters is the Executive Director of Walters International Speakers Bureau, a professional lecture agency which provides speakers world-wide to companies such as Lockheed, IBM, and AT&T. Lilly is also a private speech consultant to executives, professional trainers, and speakers.

Whether you are an "intrapreneur" in a big company, an independent agent or an entrepreneur running your own business, this book will give you some smiles and—we hope—some great ideas to apply to yourself and your business.

No matter what your situation, never believe that you work for someone else. We all work for the clients of the firm that pays us. Promotions and opportunities go to those in big business who practice the secrets of leadership. In small businesses, which according to the United States Small Business Administration employ more people than all the big businesses put together, the same laws and tenets apply.

Our friend and neighbor Sally Rand, the famous fan dancer, was also an entrepreneur and a brilliant business-woman. We asked Sally to give us one line of advice for businesspeople of the future. Sally said,

"Tell them, 'It never happens by itself.'"

This book is not dedicated to those who endlessly scan the empty horizon waiting for their ships to come in, nor to those who never sent any out.

This book is for you
who make things happen.

Contents

SIMPLE THINGS TO BUILD RELATIONSHIPS & WIN CUSTOMERS 35

SIMPLE THINGS TO BRING IN MORE BUSINESS 77

SIMPLE WAYS TO TURN YOUR BUSINESS BRAIN ON—AND KEEP IT ON ...137

Above and Beyond 175

Resources 183

Simple Things to Improve Your Office & Your Team

#1 Location of Your Office

*"International Conglomerate Consulting, Inc., may I help you?
One moment, I'll see if he's in."*

If you need foot traffic, location is paramount.

But if you don't need foot traffic, i.e., you have a mail order or phone business, why not work from home? Henry Ford started in his garage, Laura Scudder began by making potato chips in her kitchen and Mrs. Cordelia Knott started her jams, and Estée Lauder her cosmetics, from home.

If you feel uncomfortable telling people that you are working from home or that you are really on the "wrong side of town" in an inexpensive building, you may want to consider the use of a "fancy address." There are many post office mail services and answering services on the "right side of town" that can give the illusion of a "posh" business image.

Choose a
Publicity-Smart Name

It is best if your publicity-smart business name tells your potential buyers . . .

Who you are, and
What you do.

Make sure that it also . . .

Is memorable, sticks in the mind and
Projects the image you want for your service or product.

To make it memorable, you might try to make your business name euphonic. Buyers are very fond of products that begin in "k" and "m" sounds, and end in "o" sounds. They also like things that rhyme: "Hey, Hey, It's Saturday!" A real estate appraisal form company name, "Forms and Worms," is very memorable and lends itself to all kinds of fun logos and ad gimmicks. With each order, they send out a brightly colored, free plastic "worm."

Acronyms are also easily remembered. The association for speakers bureaus uses the acronym of IGAB (International Group of Agencies and Bureaus). MADD is the acronym for Mothers Against Drunk Drivers. You *never* forget these names.

#3 Heroes Build Great Teams

When it comes to "hero-ing," you better have good people holding your horse. While you're off saving the day, that support team is keeping the horses ready and your powder dry.

Build a great team. Treat every person who works with you, and for you, with love and respect.

#4 Teach Your Family to Run a Business

Make your family part of your team. A client calling your home office and hearing, "Yeah? He ain't here now, call back," does not enhance your image as a professional and an expert.

Teach your entire family how to answer your phones. Explain about the projects you are working on. Get them excited about helping you to serve your customers.

Commission incentives for your family team are a big motivator, but praise is always best. Tell others how good they are at answering the phone when *your family can overhear you.*

1. Teach your family members a pleasant business greeting to use in answering the phone, i.e., "(your business name), how may I help you?"

2. Teach them to take messages. *Never* ask someone if they mind calling back later. Trust us—they mind! *Take a message.*

3. Teach them the words that convey concern to every customer, "She very much wants to speak to you about this. She will call you back as soon as possible."

4. Teach them to close with, "Thank you for calling us!"

#5 Praise and Reward Your Team— Make Them Feel Needed

When we read of children who form gangs to rob and pillage, we think of a young boy who was interviewed on the television news recently. Both his mother and father are blind.

The boy seemed much older than his years. He answered the reporter's questions with intelligence and authority. No sneering. No bragging. He simply told the interviewer how he handled things to help his family.

The reporter asked him if he minded carrying such responsibility. The young boy replied with a proud raise of his head,

"No sir, I am needed."

There it is. The children who run in gangs feel unwanted, unloved, but most important of all, *unneeded*. We who run businesses should remember to give responsibility to those who work for us, because they must feel NEEDED in order to grow and prosper.

It is so easy to say, "Oh, I have to do it myself if I want it done right!"

But when we do the work for them, we steal from our employees the great joy, satisfaction and dignity of being needed. When we are the boss, it is important to give those who work for us the opportunity to make decisions, to set things right, to do extra things for our customers.

Thank every person who serves you. Thank your customers. Both Dottie and Lilly have a big pile of personalized postcards with their photos on them sitting on their desks. Whenever someone shows a kindness, we send a quick thank you.

When you appreciate people, you raise them in value. When you depreciate them through criticism, you lower them in value. Praise works.

As Ken Blanchard writes in his great book, *The One Minute Manager* (Morrow Publishers, New York, NY), "Catch them doing something right!"

And then we are needed. Our job is to *praise and reward.*

#6 Leadership Quality—
Caesar's Secret

Caesar's Roman legions called to each other whenever he passed, "There goes our boss, Caesar! He is *never* discouraged."

Of COURSE the man got discouraged. The point is that he did not let his men see it. He held up their spirits and courage and his own. That's leadership.

Lord Kitchener, who won three wars for the British, was a quiet man. However, they said he knew where every man and every piece of ordinance was at all times. He didn't say much, but when he spoke, he used the "voice of command." No wonder his men followed his leadership.

When our news reporters showed General Schwartzkopf putting his arm around a wounded man to help him, the country fell in love with the general.

What does it add up to?

Leadership is the ability to see other people's achievements in brighter colors, in more intricate detail and with greater unswerving concentration than anyone else.

Leadership is the ability to shift gears quickly, to tack if the winds change.

Leadership is the savvy way to make the most of all that comes and the least of all that goes.

Leadership is having the guts to be courageous even when things are tough.

Leadership is the voice of command. It is the great loving heart.

Leaders are the ones who know where they are going.

#7 When Your "Heart" Doesn't Shine

We've been at this for two days—
and we're _only_ halfway done!

We've only been at this for two days—
and we're _already halfway_ done!

Have you ever started the day feeling positive and full of ideas, then been brought down by everyone around you talking gloom and doom? How do you keep the sunshine on?

If we take the word *discourage* apart, we find *dis* means not, *cour*, from the French, means heart. So *discourage* literally means having no heart.

Here are some ideas you might like to apply next time you are faced with a flood of those "everything is terrible" remarks.

1. Keep a notebook and write down every good and positive thing you read, see or hear.

2. Respond to each "it's rotten" remark with a positive alternative. Say, "I see your point of view, but I know *you* will find a wonderful solution to that problem."

3. Ask, "How do you plan to solve that?" or ". . . earn that?"

4. Answer, "Thanks for telling me that news. Let's think of several ways we can use it to advantage!"

5. Remember, some people find their only satisfaction in life as harbingers of exaggerated bad news. You may need to free this person to work elsewhere.

In a life of business, there is no cure for gloom like the satisfaction of good work. So, *get away* from the negative group, and work with a will on a positive project. There is great wellness in the beat, rhythm and achievement of work well done. Be an example to those around you.

#8 What Tasks Are Beneath "The Boss"

As a young girl, Dottie worked at the *Los Angeles Times*. Her boss—Mildred Resstorm—was a wonderful woman who was and still is Dottie's ideal businessperson. One day in the powder room, Dottie saw Michelle take a paper towel and clean the wash basin after she washed her hands. She thought, "Oh, that work is beneath my boss. She shouldn't do that!" Then Dottie realized. Michelle did it because she was *proud* of every least thing about the *Los Angeles Times*.

Today, we run several businesses and have created and sold others. Remembering that *L.A. Times* boss, Dottie's method is to pitch in. She has a special reason for doing this. Each time, we learn new things about the ability and creativity of employees that you find out only by working with them side by side.

The mind works as the hands do, thinking of better ways to do the job. You never help your staff with a project without both of these benefits occurring.

Sandra Day O'Conner said, "Do the best you can in every task, no matter how unimportant it may seem at the time. No one learns more about a problem than the person at the bottom."

We disagree with Sandra about any task being unimportant or that we have "bottom" people in our company. However, Sandra is right that you learn about a task by doing it.

Ray Kroc of McDonald's says, "Everyone we hire is a management trainee." Maybe that is why McDonald's has a day when only the supervisors and managers do all the jobs working with customers. We believe they have found, as we have, that we always learn something new!

So next time you have an emergency, roll up your sleeves and give it a try. Keep a pad and pen handy for all the great ideas for improvement that will flash into your mind.

#9 Lead by Example

Dr. Edson Bueno is Chairman of the Board of the Amil Groupo, a $900 million company. In eight short years, it has become the fastest-growing company in Brazil. It owns hospitals, the second largest health insurance company in South America and several other businesses. Dr. Bueno has now entered the United States as the head of a chic restaurant chain in Southern California.

In interviews about their group's amazing success, Dr. Bueno's team all gave the same assessment of Dr. Bueno—he leads by example. He took a group of us to dinner at one of his restaurants; we pulled up at 11:00 p.m.

The hostess, noting that one of the owners was standing in the parking lot, came right out to greet us. "Dr. Bueno! Welcome! Are you coming in?"

"Is it too late to have dinner?"

"Dr. Bueno," she said with a smile, "We will prepare *anything* you like!"

"Ah, but this is not right," he replied with an equally big and charming smile, "What would any other customer be served at this time of night?"

"Well, appetizers and salads."

"Then we would love to join you for appetizers and salads."

As Ralph Waldo Emerson said, "Who you are speaks so loudly I can't hear what you're saying."

I soon can learn to do it if you'll let me see it done; I can watch your hands in action,
but your tongue too fast may run. And the lecture you deliver may be very wise and true,
But I'd rather get my lessons by observing what you do; For I might misunderstand you
and the high advice you give, But there's no misunderstanding how you act and how you live.

—Edgar A. Guest, 1881

#10 Use Outside Services Rather than Increase Payroll

"Yes Mrs. Smith, you'll have it tomorrow as promised, our printing department is sending it to shipping right now. Thank you for calling!"

Don't hire employees!

What?

Well, don't necessarily hire employees. Consider secretarial services, graphic artists, bookkeepers, CPAs and others who can be obtained on a per-job basis. No withholding taxes. No vacations or sick leave. For a small business, this is often a wonderful way to get started. Many will pick up and deliver work, and when work gets slow, you don't have the terrible dilemma of who to fire.

#11 Be Accessible

"Yes, they're all shipped and ready to go! You'll have them tomorrow."

How easy is it to find you? Yes, yes—you think you're easy to locate all the time, after all, *you* always know where you are. On those few occasions that your clients mention you are *a bit* difficult to locate, did you just quickly dismiss them as hard to please?

Bad call! PAY ATTENTION. Make it easy for them to buy. We live in an information age that provides all kinds of ways to keep you accessible to your clients. Perhaps a pager or cellular phone with an answering service, maybe an answering machine with remote access for you to pick up messages. How about answering services, fax machines in your car, voicemail? Bring your lap-top computer with you and use an on-line service for your e-mail. Whatever it takes in your special case: Be accessible.

If they can't find you easily, they use whomever they *can* find.

#12 Set Up a Sensible Phone System—Faxes & Phones

"Grandma, then we went swimming—oh wait, someone is calling, hang on. . ."

If you work a great deal on the phone, you will need at least three phone lines: two for your incoming and outgoing calls, and one for your fax. When you are on your first line, have your calls rotate from your first line either to your second—where you have set up an answering machine—or to your answering service. The phone companies in most cities now supply a message center that will do this automatically.

Yes, we know all about those handy switcher devices that automatically switch incoming faxes over to your fax machine if you have only one phone line. We work with more than 200 entrepreneurs weekly; some have the switcher devices, some don't. We would like to state, for the record, we HATE every one of those switcher devices we have had to work with!

If you're in business, you need to be on your phone, which means your fax is then unusable. If the fax is on the phone, *you* are unusable!

#13 Call Waiting, Answering Machines, Services, Message Services, Beepers, E-mail

In your quest to remain easily accessible, you are going to need help. Technology is speeding forward so rapidly that our suggestion on what is best will be obsolete by the time this book gets to press. Check with your local phone company for the newest options available to you. Here are a few things to keep in mind . . .

Call Waiting: Call waiting is for the *home* phone of the *non*professional. With it you must tell your caller, "Oh wait, I have another call coming in." Then comes the choice: Which one do you tell "Oh, I must take this other IMPORTANT CALL"? Either way, someone is offended.

Answering Machines: If you choose this option, get an answering machine that is voice-activated, so that it does not cut off your customers in the middle of a thought. It is terrible to get only part of a phone number or address. DO NOT have music or unprofessional answering material. Use your own voice. Make it short. Make sure you get a machine that lets you retrieve your messages from anywhere.

Services: The good news is that people much prefer to talk to real people. The bad news is, when a customer calls and says to your service, "What?!! He's not in. Great! This is just terrific, that son of a _____! Oh, just tell that idiot to call John Jones." The message you will receive from the attendant who finally gives it to you (which is rarely the person who took it) is, "Call John Jones."

Message Services: How many answering machines have you purchased in the past three years? Too many? We have, too. The phone company now has a message service system than sounds just like your answering machine—your voice, your message. It is part of a phone company computer and never breaks down—well, if it does, they take care of it. Also, when you are on the phone, you have the option of your calls being automatically transferred to the message service. Your customer never gets a busy signal. You can retrieve these calls from anywhere.

Beepers: Are better than nothing—and are getting better all the time. Some can reach you around the country and are used by an 800 number for your client's convenience.

Cellular Phones: Lilly's has a messaging/mailbox service on it. If she's on that phone, it automatically goes to a recording of Lilly saying she's on the phone or away from it, and to *please* leave her a very detailed message so she can respond quickly.

E-mail: Electronic mail will soon replace most "snail mail" (regular mail). The advantages of E-mail are many. First, it's cheaper: usually you pay only for a local call on your on-line service, plus a small monthly charge. Second, when you use E-mail you have real usable text that you can use in your documents. It saves a ton of typing.

#14 Choosing an Answering Service

Most businesspeople are now trained to use answering devices, but if your client base is of a type that still dislikes talking to a machine, use a service that has a real person.

We have used many. To test if they are worthy of your patronage, call their joint-user number yourself and see if they answer "Hello-Hold."

How long do they leave you on hold? Count how many rings it takes them to answer before the "hello-hold." Are their voices warm and friendly? The way they sound to you is the way they will sound to your clients.

Once you decide on a service, make friends with them. Thank them often. Send them gifts (candy, etc.). Their service to you will improve dramatically.

#15 Avoid Telephone Tag—What the "Electronic You" Says

"She'll be very sorry she missed your call, but please, leave a detailed message."

You don't want anyone to leave just a phone number and name on your phone answering system. You want to get back to them with the full information they want. If you don't choose an answering service, you will have some kind of electronic assistance to remain accessible to your clients. Here are some suggested words the "electronic you" might say:

"Hello, this is _____! I am out helping a customer right now. I look forward to helping you, too! Please leave me a detailed message so when I call you back I can have exactly the information you require. Take as long as you need to tell me how I may best help you today. I'll be back to you in just a little while. I want to hear all about what you need and want. Talk to you soon!"

#16 Surviving the Voicemail Maze

Here are ideas to help you break the voicemail barrier. Like you, we hate the long menu of "punch" and "pound" voicemail instructions. Touch the wrong combination and you must call back and start all over, or you get caught in a Neverneverland loop and get lost forever—a scene from your worst science-fiction nightmare—often when you are calling long distance. Exasperating! Try these ideas.

1. Ask your customers for their private voicemail extension number, which eliminates going through that miserable punch menu.
2. Ask customers for their fax number. Fax ahead to set up a telephone time when you will call.
3. When you reach a voicemail device, concentrate on your goals.
4. Use your voice! Leave a *magnificent message.*
5. Visualize: Pretend you are looking right at your prospect. Smile! Make your voice pleasant and melodic, not droning or hurried.
6. Start with a compliment. Once when Dottie was trying to reach a prospect who did not return several messages, she tried again, this time commenting on *his friendly recorded voice.* He called back in 10 minutes!
7. Offer three benefits on your message—a gift, a lead or perhaps information that you will give when the prospect calls back.
8. Talk about HIM—not about YOU!
9. Leave a choice of two times when you are available to take the return call—call it a telephone appointment.

If your prospect does not call back? He may have a deadline or be out sick or on vacation; his machine may have garbled your call or may not have worked. Go through the maze and see if the operator will give you some clues. Ask if there is another phone number or if she could page the prospect for you.

Persist with a different message each time.

#17 Answer the Phone with a Song

"Toria dora, tella me some-a mora . . ."

Well, not really. But teach yourself and your team how to use inflection in your voices when you say "hello." Train them to say, "Thank you for calling us!" The tone at the end should be up the musical scale, not down.

#18 When You Use the Phone, Put a Mirror by Your Desk

A mirror reflects how you sound as well as how you look. Most of us prefer to project a positive attitude. One glance at a mirror and you will usually change your outward attitude so you look good—to you. Strange as it sounds, that will change the image you project on the phone. You'll feel better inside, look better outside and sound better to your clients.

#19 Keep Several Pads on Your Desk

Dottie likes to use the $8\frac{1}{2}$" $\times$ 11" version with yellow lined paper.

Head up each one with the name of an article, speech or product you are planning. Ideas will come to you as you wait on the phone or are speaking to someone. Jot them down. Don't lose them.

Many computers now have "note pad" systems that are quickly accessible from any program you are working in. These are just as effective *IF* you are on your computer all day. If you must go over to your computer, turn it on, and launch the correct program, you may get interrupted or lose the idea before you can write it down.

Keep one pad by your bed. Often a great idea will come to you in the middle of the night. Grab it! Write it down.

Simple Things to

Build Relationships

& Win Customers

#20 Start Each Day with Ben Franklin's Prayer— ". . . Success of My Friends . . ."

"Thank you Lord for the *success of my friends,* and *the fewness of my enemies!* May all my friends achieve their fondest dreams . . ."

#21 Price High or Low?

Are you going to sell huge numbers of your product or service? Then price it low. If only a few can buy, then make it the fanciest possible. Elite. Posh. And price it high.

#22 Ask Everyone You Meet for a Business Card

When they give it to you, look at it. Remember, a business card is an extension of the person. Handle theirs with great respect. Let them see you put it into your wallet. Ask them for a second one to pass on to someone who will be especially interested in them. *Then do it.*

If you have to choose, it is more important to get their cards than to give yours.

#23 When in Doubt, Take a Survey

Taking a survey sets you up as "the expert." Tom Peters is possibly the most famous example of this with his now famous book, *In Search of Excellence.* He interviewed and surveyed hundreds of major businesses before writing his book.

Establish the questions your target customers most need the answers to. Develop these into a short survey—as short as possible, maybe five easy-to-answer questions. Then call on 200 of the most successful businesses that you feel may have the answers.

Not only will you now be the "expert with the answers," you will also be able to use the answers to write articles and make speeches—which further sets you up as the person to call when expert help is needed.

#24 Do What You Say You Will Do

Never let people worry and wonder: Call them. Write. Let them know you care enough not to let them wait. Don't be a no-show. Be reliable. Be on time. This one trait will build your career. Everyone will want to work with you, because you can be counted on.

Cost is nothing; value is enormous.

#25 Who Are Your Competitors?

If you want a raise, a promotion, new customers, new business partners . . . figure out who you are competing against. Once you figure out their moves, you can zoom ahead just by being "more" than your competitor.

Example: If all the shops in your area are open five days a week, what would happen if you opened for seven days? Or what if you stayed open 24 hours a day to take care of all the working men and women? If they have discontinued giftwrapping, can you offer it?

#26 Out-Think Your Competition

A beauty-parlor owner in California was scared by a new competitor who put up a huge sign saying "$6 Haircuts!" Then he thought about it and put up a sign on his building: "We *FIX* $6 Haircuts."

Whatever your competitor does, do it better. Whatever they neglect to do, do it, and do in a wonderful way! When they close, you open. Be there at the time your clients really need it done.

#27 If Your Competitor Gives Two, Give Four!

When Dottie was a little girl, an ice cream store put up a big sign, "4 Scoops for 5 Cents" (the owner was actually selling sherbet instead of ice cream). His four scoops seemed gigantic! None of Dottie's little friends had a nickel, except her. She had worked hard to save 10 cents to get to the Saturday movie. She saw the children looking longingly in the window of the store. She went in, bought a four-scoop cone, came out and sold it to her friends for a penny a lick. She collected 17 cents, then took jacks, paper dolls and other things. Of course she had to work fast because the merchandise melted!

Can you buy something big and sell it in small packages or sell something different and give far more than your competitors do?

#28 Study Your Customers

When Dottie spoke in Tokyo recently, she was scared to death because she knew a famous speaker who had a difficult time there. So Dottie did several library searches of the problems of Japanese businesswomen and read several books. Dottie learned Japanese businesswomen are torn between husbands and bosses. So, everything she told them in her speech was aimed at that, designed for them. She closed with her Girl Scout story, about what the salute meant to her, and then she taught them the salute. They were so quiet, Dottie thought they did not understand. But afterwards as they took pictures of her with group after group, all held up their hands, forming their fingers in the Girl Scout salute for the camera, to let Dottie know their hearts were with her.

Studying them—what pleases them, what they respect—shows your caring and respect.

#29 Praise and Reward Your Customers—Find Unusual Ways to Congratulate People

As with your home and business team, look for ways to praise and reward your customers.

Milton Gair owned the big men's-wear store in Redlands, California. Every morning of the year he went to the hospital, got the names of the newborn babies and filled out a gift card which he had printed for the parents. "(baby's name). Welcome to California! Please bring your folks into Gair's so we can give them a gift to celebrate your arrival." The hospital personnel handed out the cards for him. No postage. Long remembrance.

#30 Blarney or Baloney?

Does it always pay to tell the TRUTH in business?

Should we be brutally truthful or charmingly tactful?

It is a classic argument. Have you ever heard someone say, "I'm always frank." Translation: "I don't care who I hurt, I tell the brutal truth as I see it."

The old saying that "You catch more flies with honey than you do with vinegar" is true. However, being charmingly tactful requires finesse. Not "baloney," but "blarney."

The Irish say *baloney* is an unvarnished lie.

While *blarney* is the varnished truth.

A bit of Irish wisdom from Bob Walters (Dottie's husband, Lilly's father):

If, when you talk to an older woman, you say, "You have the same flawless beauty as a 17-year-old," that's baloney. She doesn't believe it, and neither did you. However, if you said, "Ah, now that I have met you, I know the age that a women becomes the most fascinating," that's blarney. A varnished truth.

You see, real beauty is in the eye of the beholder. There is something you can find to admire in everyone. When we all look for that in everyone we meet—and let them know we see it—what a nice place the world will be!

#31 "Interested" Is Irresistible

Counselors, psychologists and psychiatrists make billions of dollars each year because people in general are rather rotten listeners. These professionals will tell you their main job is just to listen.

When the great actress Sarah Bernhardt lost her leg in an accident, she bravely continued her career on the stage. When her theatrical company arrived at a new city, a newspaper editor told a young reporter to go out to interview her.

He didn't want to go. He said, "She is a *has-been*—ugly, old!" He went reluctantly.

When he came back, he excitedly wrote a glowing story about Sarah for his newspaper.

The savvy editor asked the young man, "What did you and Sarah Bernhardt talk about?"

He replied, "Come to think it, she didn't say much. But every time I said something, she leaned forward with a smile, looked into my eyes, and said, "And then?"

Eyes interested in someone, ears listening to someone, hands making notes as someone talks . . . are irresistible.

In conversations, try for being interest*ed*, rather than interest*ing*.

#32 Questions Are the Answers

"May I help you?"

When a seeker of truth asked a wise old person, "What is the answer?" a strange reply was given, "Questions are the answers."

Mysterious? Not really. Try asking some gentle and caring questions when you speak to your next customer.

A woman went into a hardware store to buy a hammer. Two were displayed: one light and inexpensive, the other strong and heavy, with a much higher price.

She asked the clerk, "What is the difference between these hammers?"

He smirked. "About $15."

He projected only his own supposed superiority. The difference was not in the price, it was in how she needed to use the hammer.

He lost the sale—not only of the hammer, but also of all the other things that woman had planned to buy in the store that day.

She went elsewhere. Will she ever recommend his store to her friends? Would you?

Many big stores now have greeters right at their front doors. After they smile and say hello, they ask, "May I help you locate what you need?" What a difference!

In serving customers, questions are the answers to building a business.

#33 Closing Negotiations and Sales

"Would you prefer to use a check or credit card?"

Before you leave a customer, close the sale! Always assume that they will buy and finish with, "When shall we deliver that?"

Do not close with a question they can answer with a yes or no (a closed-end question) such as, "Do you want to buy that?"

Close with an open-ended question that gets them thinking about how they will use and enjoy your product or service. Go over the choices with your customer, using adjectives rich with color. Quickly write down what they choose, and move to the next decision. Visualize them using the product happily. When it's all done ask, "Would you prefer to use a check or a credit card?"

#34 Ask Everyone You Meet about Their Dream

"What's your dream?"

The song from the musical *South Pacific* says, "If you ain't got a dream—how you gonna make a dream come true?"

Cecil Rhodes, one of the most successful businessmen of the last century, met people who came out to Rhodesia looking for opportunity with the question, "What's your dream?" If they had none, he didn't hire them.

Asking your clients about their dreams shows that you care. It also gives you one more avenue to help them and bond with them.

#35 To Reach Your Goals, Draw out Other People's Hopes and Dreams

"I'm the one!"

Rev. Bob Richards is an Olympic gold medalist in pole vaulting and a national decathlon champion. He often speaks to high school students on motivation. He told us he would often conclude a presentation by saying: "There is an Olympic champion right here in this auditorium! One of you is willing to pay the price. You know who you are. Thank you."—and he'd walk off the stage.

"After many speeches, some little, least likely to succeed, fat, short, skinny or underdeveloped kid would come up and say to me, "Mr. Richards, I'm going to be an Olympic champion!" Or, "I'm going to win a gold medal in four years. I'm the one!" And many of those unlikely kids were "the ones." They believed they could do it. They answered the call and went on to become Olympic champions."

—Rev. Bob Richards
(from Lilly Walters "Secrets of Successful Speakers"
© 1993, McGraw-Hill)

Draw out the dreams and goals and hopes of all you meet.

#36 Never Make the Mistake of Thinking You Work for Someone Else

As a businessperson, Dottie often volunteers to speak for the Work & Learn classes at our local schools. When she tells the kids the ageless adage, "Never make the mistake of thinking that you work for someone else," they often ask, "What do you mean?" She explains that all of us work for our customers. "If they don't come back, whatever business you work for won't be there long."

Then she tells the kids to think of how to do these three things at work that day.

1. Look for a way to give your boss a hand without asking for praise or reward.

2. Think of ways to make your company's customers smile.

3. Think of ways the company can save money—and make more money.

Then, she promises the young people that if they will do these three things every day, they will become the owners of businesses, leaders of industry. There will be no stopping them in their business careers!

Some laugh, some look bored, but sometimes she sees that flash of intelligence in their eyes. She closes by saying, "You who understand are America's future business champions. *You know who you are.*"

#37 Be Proud

Have you ever thought how important it is to find something to be proud of?

Marva Collins, a wonderful teacher, says there is nothing to be proud of when we teach little children to read books that say "Run, Jane run." So she starts every class, from first grade up, with Ralph Waldo Emerson's essay, "Self-Reliance." The children love it.

Did you see the wonderful movie *Stand and Deliver* about the East Los Angeles math teacher Jaime Escalante? He taught failing high school students calculus and coached them to pass the National Advanced Placement Calculus Exam.

One line caught our hearts. Mr. Escalante says, "You kids are winners! You have math in your blood! Your ancestors were Aztecs and Mayans. You are mathematical wizards, astronomers!"

Every successful organization gives their employees, members, customers and citizens something to be very proud of. Think about it today. What can you do to enhance the things about your company that will make all of you proud, that will make people proud to work with you, buy from you and know you?

#38 Visualize Success: Yours, Your Company's, Your Customer's

One day Dottie picked up an advertising sales trainee. On the way, Dottie heard a new Chevron gas station ad on the radio. Dottie said to the trainee, "Let's go and see him. He is looking for business."

"Why?" the beginner replied. "He certainly doesn't need us."

Dottie went anyway. As Dottie drove into the station the trainee said, "He won't be here." He poked his head in Dottie's car window with a big smile and said, "I'm the owner, may I fill it up?" Dottie said, "I can visualize many customers coming into this beautiful station. May I talk to you about them, as you pour my gas?" "Sure!" he grinned. Dottie nudged the trainee. "Get out and watch me close this sale." She said, "Why? He has plenty of advertising now." She didn't get out. Dottie did. He bought. Dottie fired the trainee.

Visualize *their* success and often you help yourself achieve *your own* success.

#39 Visualize Your Clients as the People They Wish They Were

Use phrases such as "a smart person like you" or "someone with your pep and enthusiasm." Vince Lombardi, the famous coach, said, "In each player's heart is a dream and a hurt. When I look at the hurt, a synergy takes place and the hurt grows. Pretty soon the player can think of nothing else and drops out. When I speak only of the dream, the goal, a different synergy takes place. It blazes, sparkles. Soon the hurt is forgotten! Therefore, I only talk of dreams."

#40 Help Customers Visualize How Happy They Can Be

"Wow, you look great in turbo!"

As customers got in the car for a test drive, a successful car dealer said, "Wait a minute, you look so good in this car!" Let me show you!" He held up the mirror so that they could see themselves as the prosperous, successful, happy OWNERS OF A NEW CAR.

When they bought, he took a picture, and asked them for a satisfied customer testimonial. He put these up together on his wall. It made customers feel important and let buyers see how happy his other customers were.

#41 Smile

Look into the eyes of every person you meet and smile. Costs nothing. Makes you look great, makes them feel great.

Smiling is the most inexpensive cosmetic on earth.

#42 Ask the Referrals for Referrals

The whole concept of networking is branching out your business from one business to the next, one person to the next. Don't break the chain.

Thank everyone who gives you a referral.

Ask them for another.

When you call the referral, say, "Bill suggested that I call. I would love to help you find what you need."

#43 Just Say "No" to Business

"Well, maybe if you put the ice cream in a small bowl. No. No ice cream. Bring me the wine menu again."

What!?

Ever hear of the 80/20 Rule? That you get 80% of your business from 20% of your clients?

We think you also get 80% of your heartaches from only 20% of your clients.

After a while you will have an immediate feel for those clients who will be nothing but trouble. When you feel one of those approaching, don't be afraid to very nicely "just say no." Better yet, sweetly refer them to one of your competitors. With any luck your competitor has the right personality "chemistry" to avoid those hassles and heartaches you know you would have generated had you attempted to assist this client.

The customer then has a better chance of finding what they want, and your competitors think you're terrific. More important, you have more time to service those clients who *do* generate income—that golden 20% at the top.

Warning: Do not be rude or unprofessional to those you feel might not be part of that 20%, but do give them your competitor's phone numbers. They might have a better rapport. Everyone wins.

#44 Leave the Door Open

"That's OK Mr. Brown. Next year we'll have even more flavors!"

It is awkward when customers must tell you they don't want you or your product. You will get "no's." You will get angry customers, but look for ways to leave the door open.

Try to make them feel good, and you will see them again.

The Holiday Inns were begun when Kemmons Wilson was turned down by every bank when he asked for start-up loans. He raised money elsewhere and began his business. Then he went back to the original banks and did business with them, too. He could do this because he always "left friends."

Simple Things to Bring in More Business

#45 There Are Only Two Kinds of Prospects

1. Those who are customers now: Find more ways to help them. Ask them for referrals.

2. Those who are not customers YET! Find them. Ask them for referrals.

#46 Where Do You Find Buyers?

1. The library

2. Your phone book

3. Friends and acquaintances of your buyers

4. The associations that your buyers belong to

5. Through every piece of mail

6. Trade journals

Can you think of other places?

#47 Listen & Observe: The Greatest Secret of a Successful Business

"Find a need and fill it." How? Simply listen to and observe those around you who say they have a need, can't find something or are coping with a problem. Then think: how many people or businesses have this same problem? Will your idea make money for them or save them expenses? Investigate others solving the problem now. Do you have a new angle on a unique solution?

Ask gentle questions. Bruce Barton, the great advertising genius, said, "Put on the role of the humble inquirer." Listen to the customer's voice, watch the face, get into the mind. See what hurts—and what pleases. See the dream. Then it is simple to become a "buyer's assistant." Your job is to help your customers get what they want.

Bill Marriott had a restaurant in Washington, D.C. One day a waitress complained about "those darn travelers, always wanting me to make up meals to bring on the planes. Such a big bother." Marriott listened and observed. Ever wonder who makes most of those meals on planes now? Look out your plane window at those trucks bringing in the food, all owned by Marriott! Those little Host restaurants in most airports? Marriott again.

Ben Franklin wrote in every letter and article, "I observed."

Harry Heinz saw his mother cry while grating fresh horseradish for his father. Horseradish is much worse than onions. He got the idea of grating horseradish by machine. That product started his 57 varieties.

What is hurting your customers?

Listen and observe those who buy from you and those who don't.

#48 Can You Sell the Negative?

Diane Reed was an out-of-work publicist who had just opened her own office after her longtime boss died. She took a survey of every business in her building, asking what their greatest problem was. All said, "We are afraid of being robbed." Because she was short of funds, she kept thinking, "no money." She put the two needs together. She sent out press releases to the media offering to give "No Money On Board" window stickers for store, truck and bus windows free to any merchant who had the problem. She was deluged with people who wanted stickers. She asked each recipient to fill out a "Publicity Needs Survey" with their name, address and phone number and thus gained more business than she could handle.

At a gas station on the way to the desert, the sign read, "Last stop before the desert. Don't die out there, fill up on our *Free Water!*" Everyone stops. Business thrives.

#49 Can You Make It Easier or Cleaner?

The Mars Company has made a fortune and became the largest candy company in the world by coating chocolate with beeswax and using the slogan, "It melts in your mouth, not in your hands."

Can yours be easier or cleaner than your competitor's?

#50 You May Be Talking to the Wrong Person

One day Dottie went out to sell four ads for the shoppers' column she wrote for a rural newspaper. All four turned her down. They said the president of the Chamber of Commerce was not advertising with her, so neither would they. Without those ads, Dottie could not make the house payment. She drove to the president's drug store and went in to ask him—again—to advertise. He did not answer one word, only shook his head "No." Dottie thought, "I'm going to fail. I can't save our house." She walked toward the front of the store where there was a soda fountain and sat down. She didn't have the energy to leave. She bought a cherry Coke with her last dime and choked back tears. A lady sitting next to her kindly asked what was wrong. Dottie told her. The woman asked to read the sample of the column Dottie had brought with her. The woman seemed much more attentive to the details than might be expected. Suddenly she spun around on her stool, and called "Ruben! Come here!" The owner of the store came out. She told him to buy an ad from Dottie. He was her husband! Dottie had been talking to the wrong person. The owner was so easygoing that he always said "yes" to everyone. His wife had made him promise not to buy any more advertising! Then the wife went to the phone and called the four businesses who had turned Dottie down—they all said "yes." That day, the turning of the soda fountain stool was the turning point in Dottie's business.

That drug store was a customer of Dottie's for 25 years. When the store went modern and turned into a pharmacy only, they tore out the beautiful old soda fountain. Bob bought it for Dottie: it's right in her office today. Why don't you come by some day, and we'll give you a cherry Coke.

#51 Target Your Market, Then Be an Expert

"Now, to make the perfect doggie treat. . . ."

When people go to buy, they hope and pray they are trusting their money to a true expert. So, be that expert. Don't try to be "all things to all people," because customers will assume that a "jack of all trades is a master at none."

Lilly owns several condominiums. She has gone through several real estate agents over the years. One now holds that special place in Lilly's heart as "my real estate agent." (You'll know you have won their loyalty when they start to refer to you as "my _____.") She projects the image of a "condominium" expert. How? On all of her business cards, and letterheads it says so. Four times a year Lilly gets a newsletter with information on the condominium just within the complexes in which Lilly has property. She keeps Lilly informed on how much property is moving for, actual closed sale prices, city and state laws that might affect her property.

Target your market, then become an expert within it.

#52 Use Everything to "Promote"

CAUTION: CONTENTS OF ENVELOPE MAY CAUSE LAUGHTER

On the outside of your envelopes, the bottom of your letterhead, packaging of any kind, print information about what you are promoting and selling.

Every piece of mail requires postage—use that investment to the fullest! Print an attractive order form and include it in everything you send out.

Dale Irvin, famous professional humorist, has "Caution: Contents of envelope may cause laughter" on his envelopes. There is no doubt he is promoting the sale of laughter.

#53 Leave a Trail They Can Follow Back to You

Everything you send out should leave a trail the customer can follow back to you. There are literally thousands of promotional items you can use: pens, magnets, balloons. . . .

Whatever you decide on, make it:

1. Something *your* customers need to use often.

2. Something that points back to your company. It must at minimum have your name and phone number.

Consider giving away something that can be printed on a single sheet of paper like: "Ten Rules" or "15 Things to Avoid" (of course these things are about your product or service). It only costs you one piece of paper, and if done on a pretty piece of paper, might even get hung up on their wall.

One company provided free color postcards with a scene of their community for their customers to mail to their friends—of course on the back were the words "courtesy of (their company)."

#54 Try Postcards Instead of Letters

Use postcards to acknowledge an order, to remind your clients that you are thinking of them or to say "Thank you." Less postage, no envelope, no secretary involved. Keep them with you at all items, with your address book. Write them while you wait for a plane or when you're on a phone call.

Besides, do you read *every* piece of mail, *all* the way through? Neither do we. Do you always read those brief hand-written notes from people? So do we!

#55 Put Order Blanks in Everything

Put order blanks for everything you do—in everything! Put order blanks in other orders, your newsletter, your letters, etc.

Take advantage of every opportunity to make it easy for your customer to buy again.

#56 Put Your Picture on Everything You Print

First, you sell *you*, second your service or product. Everything you print with your company name should have your picture. People will identify you—the real, breathing, caring person—with what you offer them.

#57 Make New-Prospect Calls Every Day

Hello! We wanted you to know we are just down the street!

Don't get so wrapped up in the old business that you neglect your future. Set a reasonable goal for yourself in your business. Talk to new prospects every day. For a telephone solicitor it might be 50 new prospects, for a speakers bureau salesperson perhaps five. Set a goal and stay with it.

#58 Make a New Deal Every Day

It's better to do something for nothing than nothing for nothing. Daily, if you don't make a cash sale, make *some* kind of action happen in your business. How about trading your products or services for a gift or prize for your staff? Or "Thank you's" to your customers? Make a coupon-exchange deal with another business. In return, they give you an evening out.

Don't let a day go by without making a positive forward stride.

#59 Keep Your Eyes Open for Every Piece of Advertising

NEVER call it junk mail. Your mail box and fax are the bazaars of the world. Study each ad. Ask yourself if you can sell your seminars, your services or your products to that company. The fact that they advertise shows that they are eager for business.

Look at the advertisement and ask yourself:

1. Can you help this business?

2. Can you team up with them on their next advertising or promotional venture?

3. Can you refer clients to them and receive clients in return?

4. Look at the layout of their advertising piece. Study it. Is it good? Then keep it in a file so that when you redo your materials you can refer to it for ideas. Is it bad? Then learn what not to do.

5. What about the offer in the ad? Could you use a version of it for your customers? Does the ad offer a combination, a deadline, a gift with every order?

Learn.

#60 Before You Open Your Wallet, Open Your Mind

THINK: Am I purchasing this from one of *my* clients? If so, be sure to let the client know you are a customer. This will warm your buyer's heart and make him or her want to continue doing business with you.

THINK: Ask yourself, "Where can I use my purchase to help me start a new relationship with a new prospect for my own business? Use your purchase to open a new door.

THINK: Can you offer a trade of your services or products for theirs? If you can, you have a new client and a better bank balance all at the same time! Business begets business.

#61 Team Up with a Complementary Business

Can you combine your efforts with a complementary business to advertise?

The multimillion dollar wedding business is a good example. Often caterers, photographers, tux rental shops, florists, printers, wedding chapels and others will team up to send out invitations and hold a huge Wedding Fair for engaged couples. They are able to split the printing, the postage, the site rental, the ads and similar costs. They can even offer the buyer a big savings if they buy the "package deal," which includes use of all of the businesses. Everyone benefits.

Coupon co-op promotions are often used in retail businesses. Grocery stores print coupons for car washes and pizza places, etc. on their receipt tapes. Think of a business complementary to your own. A gym might hand out coupons for a beauty parlor, and vice versa. All of you offer a 10% discount if they shop in these other businesses or a gift with a purchase. This is a great benefit to your customers and to you! The only cost is the printing, which is split many ways.

Can you do this sort of co-op for a group in your field?

#62 Become Famous! Get It in the News

You may be surprised at what you can get in the news that obviously helps promote your business.

Sit down and look at your business. What problems does your service or product solve? Get a few statistics on that issue from the library. Now write a short press release about it: State the reasons it's bad, then state your favorite three solutions, one of which is related to what you do. Perhaps add a new angle, a way the problem could have been prevented.

It may be a while before you are a household name, but you can be a celebrity within a defined market.

Obtain names and addresses of all newspapers, magazines, TV and radio shows at your local library and from the visitors and convention bureaus, the Chamber of Commerce and the phone book.

Market yourself as an expert (by this time, of course, you have done the research and taken the survey, and you *are* an expert).

#63 Write Articles

The magazine reads: 10 TIPS AVOID CAT ALLERGIES

Once you have become an expert, write articles for the trade publications, magazines, newspapers and newsletters in your field. Send a short bio and photograph with the story. Some publications will even pay you!

Make the headline an answer to a need or problem in your area of business. "How to Solve . . ."

As with other news sources, you can't simply say why your product is great, but you can tell them all about the problems and concerns of the typical buyer (of products like yours) and then offer solutions.

Small publications that target your market are delighted to print your articles *if* they offer benefits to their readers. Target newsletters and magazines of the associations of your current and prospective customers.

If you don't like writing, try thinking of "lists." "The 10 Worst Problems (and Solutions!) for _____ ." "Six Ideas to Avoid _____ ." These are easy to write and are very valuable to your customers and the publication you write for. Case in point: You bought a book called "101 Simple Things . . ."

Also include Kipling's six honest serving men.

I had six honest serving men,
They taught me all I knew!
Their names were What *and* Where *and* When,
How and Why *and* Who!

—Rudyard Kipling

#64 Write a Book

"Oh? My autograph?"

Gather your articles together and you will have a book! A book gives you credibility and prestige. Often it can give you a nice increase in your income.

Consider a book that needs to be reprinted every year with annual information that your clients and customers will need to have to solve their problems better.

Benjamin Franklin made his fortune with his famous "Poor Richard's Almanac," which is still revised and reprinted today. An attorney publishes a book on the latest laws applying to tenants, including ideas on how to handle tenant problems. A new edition comes out each year. He has become famous while he helps his clients and makes a high profit.

#65 Self-Publish

All right—500 to pet store chain, 1,000 to airport, 1 to Aunt Sally. . . .

Sometimes businesspeople who write valuable books or create audio or video products have difficulty finding the right publisher. They may not have approached publishers whose market is ideal for their subject. Perhaps the subject is so narrow that publishers believe they cannot sell enough copies to make a profit. One possible answer to this dilemma is self-publishing.

Many famous authors began by self-publishing. Dan Poyntner loved hang gliding. He knew that market inside out. But no book publisher would consider his book because of the narrow market for it. So Dan self-published it and has made a fortune. He is now known as the world expert on the subject, not only of hang gliding but also of self-publishing. He sells his book to airports, hang gliding shops, clubs and through direct mail.

Consider publishing the "Handbook on. . ." (whatever problem your clients buy your product or service to solve). Your ideas—in a simple printed format—can make life easier for your clients . . . and might bring you fame and fortune!

#66 Publish a Newsletter

It can be yearly, quarterly or monthly. Start with one double-sided, legal-sized sheet. Have an artist design an interesting logo for you. Put your picture on it. Send it to customers to remind them of you. Interview your clients and print stories about them. Print stories about new services and products (of course the ones you offer!) and ideas on how to use them. Put these newsletters out on your counter, include them in orders, send them to editors who may pick up some of your material.

#67 Be a Speaker

What if you could speak to groups who could become customers or clients for your business or practice? You would be addressing a ROOM FULL OF PROSPECTS.

This is how Dottie began her businesses. Dottie had no car or money, so she used an invaluable resource, *an idea*. She noticed that she often couldn't reach her prospective clients—business owners—since they always seemed to be at their service clubs hearing some speaker. Speaker? Bingo! She developed a talk about "Customer Service." During the talk, Dottie collected business cards in a little basket so that she could give away a prize by having a drawing. Thus, she also brought home a basket full of leads.

By this means she built an advertising business with 285 employees, four offices and 4,000 continuous contract advertising accounts.

Create a 20-minute talk on the latest feature of your industry, new trends, a problem (and the solutions) that your customers often face.

Use lots of stories and clean humor. Then call local service clubs and offer to do your talk for free. At the talk, ask attendees to fill out evaluation sheets with their names, addresses and phone numbers on them. (If you hold a drawing using those sheets and give a gift as a prize, most people will fill them out for you.) Many businesses have been built in this way. Once people hear you speak, they place you in their thoughts as an authority.

Have you stepped into a hotel and noticed the posted list of all the meetings going on that day? Think of the conference and convention centers in every major city in the world . . . and how long *their list* of daily events must be.

Think. CAN YOU SPEAK TO PROMOTE YOUR BUSINESS? Can you make your talk fun and informative? *If so,* you can promote your business beyond your wildest dreams with no investment of money—just the investment of your ideas, hopes and helpfulness. Yes, there is money in your mouth and gold on the tip of your tongue!

#68 Secrets of Professional Speakers to Overcome Stage Fright

"No way am I going to try and be a speaker!"

Feeling a bit of stage fright? Would you like a few secrets professional speakers use to overcome stage fright?

If you have felt your mouth go dry, your knees shake and your heart beat so hard you thought the audience must surely hear it, here are some ideas to help you give a star performance.

1. As you stand off stage waiting to be introduced, visualize each person in the audience as being hungry. Each holds an imaginary empty bowl. Then picture yourself carrying a huge tray of the most delicious food. Each dish is their favorite. When you step forward to the lectern, you say to them mentally, "Here I am! I have just what you are hungry for!"

2. Don't try to memorize a speech. Make an outline.

3. Ways to begin: Ask a question; make a historical reference; quote a dictionary definition; repeat famous or unusual quotes, songs, poems or rhymes. Anything unexpected will do. Make a promise; use humor (but only if it helps to bring the main message you want to get across to your audience).

4. Don't try to make too many points. Consider three.

5. Use stories to illustrate each of the three points, then repeat the points. Project your stories upon the theater of their minds, feel the stories as you tell them. See the story as you tell it.

6. Close with a great heart story. This often brings the audience to their feet with a standing ovation. A story of the human spirit overcoming great odds, a story of someone in their industry or from your own life.

#69 Become a Paid Speaker

". . . and how much is your fee to teach my sales team to appreciate cats?"

Dottie built her entire advertising business by speaking without charging a fee. One day one of the merchants asked her to give the same talk for his employees. "How much is your fee, Mrs. Walters?" he asked. She gulped and asked him, "What do you have in mind?" He offered her $50 for the talk and she stepped into the World of Paid Speaking, which has taken her far and wide.

Before they offer you money, inquire about their budget for speakers and trainers. If they have none, offer to take your fee in exchange for advertising your services in their publications or media.

#70 Form a Master-Mind Group

Form a Master-Mind Group of noncompeting business friends. Meet with them once a week to talk about new ideas, solve problems, gain new opportunities and give each other leads. Great fortunes have been made with this one idea.

#71 Offer Seminars for Your Client's Customers

Offer to hold a seminar for your client's customers. Example: You sell manure. Your main customers are nursery owners, who sell it to home owners. You have learned a great deal about handling the stuff that the end-buyer might be thrilled to know. Speak to the nursery owners, offer to do a short seminar for their clients. The client pays you, they gain new customers, the customers get great information. You are further established in the minds of your clients as the one to call when they want great information.

#72 Don't Give Up, Follow Up!

"You never win if you never play."

For every five well-thought-out, good prospects you contact, four will say "no," at least temporarily. Leave the four "no's" smiling. Leave the doors open. Know for sure that there is a fifth, who is waiting for you because you have the answer to that person's problem.

Sometimes it takes 20 prospects to reach the four sales, and all four sales come in the last five contacts. It is a matter of odds. To get the odds weighed in your favor, you must accept the invitation to speak to 20 prospects. The results will be four sales, and 16 will say, "call us back because . . ."

When you call or knock, feel your pace and rhythm. If it starts to slow, remember the odds.

When a man prayed to God to ask to win the lottery, God answered, "First you must buy some lottery tickets!"

If you try, you may not win every time.

If you don't try, you will never win. Guaranteed.

#73 How Can You Do What You Do, in a New Way?

*"You are wearing Chanel #5 at your party this evening?
No problem! Fluffy will have it on, too!"*

Take your old product and combine it, or change it slightly into something new, like a "mile-long hot dog," a hand-held TV set, a telephone watch. A man who trained dogs for dog lovers now teaches post office employees, meter readers and delivery services "How to Stop Dog Attacks."

McDonald's takes its same old shakes and just makes a slight change to mint-flavored green shakes for Saint Patrick's day!

Walter Knott crossbred a new berry to create the boysenberry and opened a pie stand along the road by his farm. Then he served chicken dinners and sold berry jam and berry pies to take home. Knott's Berry Farm became crowded with people waiting for dinner, so he built a "ghost town" and sold tickets. When Disneyland opened a few miles away, he didn't panic: he went to the travel people and promoted a "combo-tour." Knott's Berry Farm is now one of the largest amusement parks in the world.

Johann Gutenberg saw a coin punch and combined it with a wine press to invent the printing press. Joseph Strauss built a new kind of bridge in San Francisco—he saw it in a dream, a suspension bridge. Steve Jobs of Apple Computer saw a computer like a bicycle: A human moving on a bicycle is twice as efficient as a condor flying in the air, so the computer is an extension of human locomotion.

Pam Lontos, a famous speaker, broke her leg. She figured out a new telephone technique to contact her customers. She so increased her sales, her boss asked her to teach the other salespeople. She did that so well, he made her the sales manager of all their radio stations. She did that so well, she now has a sales-training business and speaks all over the world to salespeople.

Make your product or service bigger or smaller, available earlier, later or for home delivery. Do it faster, do it in a new color.

#74 Make Your Business Card Unusual

"A special gift to thank Fluffy for coming to visit us."

You have a lot of competition when your business card is just one of many dull black-and-white cards. So think of ways to make your business card different, unique. Wally Amos, the cookie man, attached a tiny sealed package containing a little cookie to his business card. People loved to eat the cookie and keep the card.

How about making your card in the shape of a Rolodex® card with a little tab listing either your name, your company name or what you do? People will keep your card because it is easy to refer to and they have somewhere to put it.

Put your picture on the card. Use lots of color. Why be dull when with a tiny bit of effort you can be delightful?

#75 Lure Customers by Offering What They Like Best

In one of Bill Marriott's first restaurant businesses, he took a fan and blew the heavenly smell of good, hot, Mexican chili out onto the cold, snowy streets of Washington, D.C. He called the restaurant the "Hot Shop." The same idea was picked up by Debbie Field, who blew the smell of those wonderful chocolate chip cookies into shopping malls. When Dottie was a little girl in Los Angeles, a taffy shop was located next to a cinema. A fan wafted that delicious smell of just-made taffy onto the street. No one went into that theater without a big bag of taffy.

Can you use any of the five senses to let your prospects know you have something great waiting for them? Use delicious words to describe benefits. Elmer Wheeler called it "Selling the Sizzle!"

#76 Can You Be Controversial?

Years ago the Chicago World's Fair was failing. The famous fan dancer Sally Rand had an idea. She used huge six-foot ostrich fans in her dance. The question: Was she wearing anything under them? She arranged for the police chief to arrest her. Her attorney arranged bail. Next day she was back at the fair. The chief arrested her again. Every newspaper in the country covered the story. The entire fair was pulled out of the red because of the publicity.

#77 Add Something Else—
Gift with Purchase

"They had a two-for-one sale! This one is all for you!"

When you offer something special with the purchase, you'll have a tried-and-true method of increasing sales.

A man with a video rental store in an area with many competitors wondered what he could offer to those who rented videos from him. All the stores had the same movies. He thought: "What goes well with movies? Popcorn!"

His wife made the best caramel popcorn you ever tasted. So he had her make up a big batch of these balls, wrapped them in saran wrap and handed one out with every rental. Soon his store was jammed! People loved the caramel corn so much he then marketed it to be sold in grocery and specialty stores and created a whole new business.

Many fast food restaurants offer two-for-one deals. Their advertising suggests that the customer use the second item as a gift. People love to give gifts.

#78 Don't Sell Singles, Sell Series

Instead of selling things one at a time, why not offer to deliver one each month, or three each quarter? That's how book-of-the-month clubs, fruit and dessert-of-the-month clubs were born. Now there is a very successful cartoon poster club for dentists who hang the humorous posters on the ceilings over their dentist chairs.

The same idea can be applied to many things: flowers of the month, earrings of the month . . . you are limited only by your imagination.

#79 Make a Value Package of Your Services or Products

Think of ways to package your products and services by combining a slow-moving item with some hot ones. Call it a *Lollapalooza,* maybe a *Grand Slam* or another kind of super-jazzy name. We know a speaker who offers $2,000 packages of his products, which have a retail value of $2,500. He sells a huge amount of them at every program to those who are "serious about their careers." Remember, it doesn't take nearly as many customers to buy the big packages for the total sales to break through the ceiling. Another speaker invites people to join his $1,000 club. They give him their credit card or check in this amount and receive products and seminar certificates worth $1,500, plus a pin saying, "I'm successful! I'm a member of the $1,000 club!"

#80 Offer Discounts for Groups

Issue a special card to seniors, Little League players, members of the Boy and Girl Scouts. Think of groups in your area who would be great customers for you and who would appreciate a special offer. Be sure that you treat them like royalty when they present their card. There is nothing worse than a reluctant offer.

Simple Ways to Turn Your Business Brain On—and Keep It On

#81 Get a Promotion Attitude

When we have a business, a practice or a career, it is our responsibility and joy to promote it. We must search out possibilities. Think of new and better ways to do things. Figure out unusual markets, packages of products and services. We have discussed many ways to be a real PRO-moter.

If we take the word apart, pro means for. A positive thought, combined with mote, the second syllable, which comes from the root "motion." Put up posters for yourself with expressions you like, such as "Carpe Diem" (*Seize the Day*), "Do It Now and Do It Better," "No More Alibis," "If It is to Be, it is Up to Me." Looking at these positive thoughts often will burn them into your subconscious until you go on automatic in a positive/creative/promotion mode. "Try It, You'll Like It!"

#82 Breakthrough Ideas— Note the Apple!

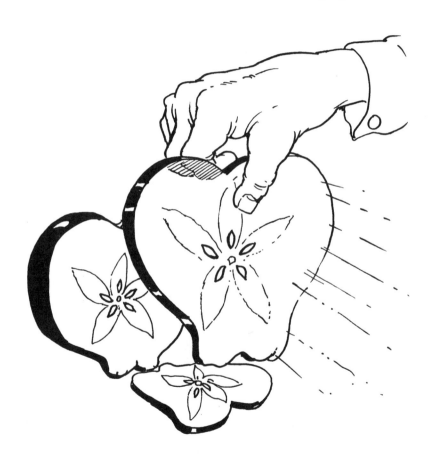

"To See Things in the SEED: That is GENIUS."
—Lao-tse, Confucius' teacher

Sometimes the reason we cannot see the solution to a problem is that we keep looking at it in the same old way. Just as we usually pick up an apple and cut it the same old way we, our parents and our grandparents have always done it. We quarter the apple, cutting it from top to bottom, right? Because we use the same method, we keep getting the same result. "If you always do what you've always done, you'll always get what you always got." But what if we sliced the apple the other way, across, into very thin, round slices?

Hold up the paper-thin slice to a light, and you will find a tremendous message waiting for you.

First you will see the outline of the apple blossom in the lovely white apple flesh. Blossoms and springtime symbolize hope.

Next, within the blossom outline, you will see a star, to remind you of summer evenings and the first lovely star upon which to make a wish.

In the center of the star are the apple seeds.

Here is the apple message. "Can you count the number of seeds?" Yes, of course you can. That isn't hard, is it? Now: Pick up one seed and hold it in the palm of your hand.

Can you count the number of trees, or the number of apples, that one seed can produce?

The infinite possibilities for solutions to problems are like seeds in your mind. Your potential is as unlimited as an apple seed. Look at your problem from another angle.

#83 Don't Have Time to Be Creative?

Have you ever felt so pressured you have said, "I just don't have TIME to get all my regular work done, let alone work on new projects. I've got to make more time!"

Really? How? We all have the same amount of time, 24 hours a day. The best you can do is to use the time you have to greater advantage. Here are some ideas to get lots more done in less time than you ever thought possible.

- Carry a tape recorder or notebook and pencil with you. Jot down ideas. Use a different page for each project so you can sort as you go.

- As you jog, work in the garden, exercise, scrub the bathroom, get dressed or drive, listen to instructional audio tapes. Steve Allen (the brilliant comedian, musician and author) says, "Turn your car into a university on wheels. Use otherwise wasted time. Bombard your mind with audio ideas from great teachers and trainers."

Don't worry about too many ideas, you haven't *begun* to use all the capability of your mind!

#84 Get the "Time to Be Creative" Attitude

In the popular TV show "MacGyver," the hero was a young man who works with impossible materials and finds news ways to "save the day." When the flood is coming, the flesh-eating ants are on the march, everything seems terrible, MacGyver grins and says, "Time to be creative!"

When you are faced with crises, rejoice. Your mind will kick into the "time to be creative" attitude. Some of your *best* ideas will come to you in the pressure of crisis.

#85 Program Your Mind to Find Solutions as You Sleep

Go over the problems of the day just before you go to sleep. Say the prayer, "I have thought of these ways to solve this problem. There is a perfect solution. I release my problem now. I am ready to act. I am opening the floodgates of the Genius River—let me be the channel." Then go to sleep.

Next morning, the solution will flash into your mind when you are least expecting it. It may be a picture, or a voice—you will recognize it! It will seem familiar. Like a good friend who comes up behind you when you are in difficulty, and says "Here I am." The Idea will grab you!

The genius river of ideas is rising! Open the floodgates!

#86 Conceive It, Believe It, Achieve It. What's Your Dream?

Hey, what's your dream?

Is it possible to visualize a dream and then make it come true? In fact, it is the only way to build dreams into reality.

If you have dreamed great dreams, then you have heard someone say to you, "Well, seeing is believing!" Meaning, "You idiot! That is just a daydream."

The truth is, nothing is achieved without a dream. Then comes believing it is possible.

Both Marcus Aurelius of ancient Rome, and Napoleon Hill, who wrote *Think & Grow Rich* centuries later, said, "If you can conceive it and believe it, you can achieve it."

That's the way every building is constructed, every bridge is built, every good thing is invented. Conceive it, dream about it, believe it, think of what it takes to build it, then achieve it. Take action.

What if it doesn't work? Just go back to those same steps and redo them.

Robert Goddard was a sickly boy who spent his time reading the science fiction of H.G. Wells and Jules Verne. After a long siege of illness he finally was allowed to go out into his back yard.

Robert climbed up in a cherry tree and day dreamed. Suddenly, he saw a huge rocket ship beside him! He studied every detail, then climbed down and asked his mother for a notebook. He sat down and sketched that rocket ship, drawing every thing his mind's eye had visualized. In high school, Robert began building rockets.

Robert Goddard became the father of modern rocketry. Every time a rocket failed, he was undaunted. Robert Goddard said, "Look how much we have learned!" They named the great U.S. rocket center for him, that silly little boy full of dreams.

#87 Plan to Win

Have you ever noticed that some folks have a small success, then seem to do everything they can to stand in their own way? They don't have a plan to *continue to win.*

Spanish conquistador Hernando Cortés conquered all of Mexico with a handful of men, a few horses and a PLAN!

The Spanish ships landed in a port they called Vera Cruz. Cortés put his plan into action. He gathered warriors from the local tribes who were tired of being tyrannized by Montezuma and his armies. Cortés organized a huge army of natives, led by his men. Then he made a master plan to march on Montezuma.

However, the Spanish soldiers were afraid. They went to Cortés and said, "Boss, your Plan A—to march on Montezuma and win, is great. But let's put together Plan B. A safe plan of retreat back to our ships."

Cortés replied that he would think it over and get back to them the next morning. In the night, Cortés sent out his personal servants to sink his own ships in the harbor!

At dawn his men were thunderstruck. "What about Plan B to retreat to the ships?" they cried. Cortés answered, "We are going with Plan A. The plan to WIN."

#88 Keep a Journal of Your Dreams and Goals

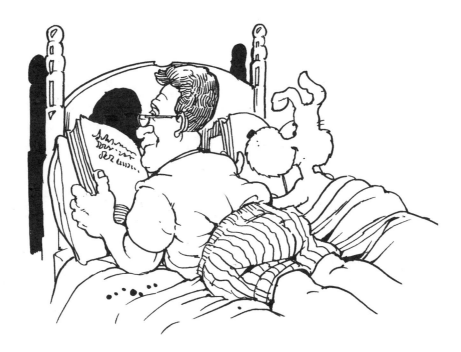

Keep a record—a journal—of each day's plans, as well as a weekly, monthly and yearly plan. You are much more likely to achieve your dreams if you write them down and review them each night before you go to sleep.

When you get discouraged, look back over your journal at all you have accomplished. Your spirit will rise, you will be ready to continue the journey.

#89 Picture It Done

Put up a picture, a figure, the words, that are the goal you intend to reach. Put it where you will see it every day.

Conrad Hilton used this method of achievement. Conrad always put up a picture of each hotel he dreamed of buying. Then he made the dream come true.

#90 Love Your Work!
Your Business, Industry, Profession

If you are in a field you don't like, don't hang around there like a dead weight around your boss's neck. Who wants to do business with, or promote, a miserable complainer? Get out and find something in which you can be swept away. Love your work so much that when they ask you how many hours a day you work, your answer is not "As few as possible," but instead, "All of them! I only wish there were more!" Confucius said, "You will never labor a day in your life when you find the work that you love passionately."

#91 Ignore Those with No Vision

And then it flew.

They told Robert Fulton when he worked on his steam boat, "It won't go, it won't go, it won't go." When it did go, the same people stood on the bank and said, "It won't stop, it won't stop, it won't stop."

The college president of a small denominational college disagreed with his bishop. The year was 1870, the bishop's assertion was that everything that could be invented had been invented. The college president exclaimed to him, "In 50 years," he said, "men will learn how to fly like birds."

The bishop, shocked, replied, "Flight is reserved for angels and you have been guilty of blasphemy."

Back home, angels were sending other dreams to the two small sons of Bishop Milton Wright—Orville and Wilbur.

The Wright brothers invited the whole town to watch their plane fly at Kitty Hawk. People signed a petition to have them incarcerated in an insane asylum. Only five people came that day to watch the most important event of the century.

And then it flew.

#92 Look Past the Problem to the Solution

To succeed in business, we must constantly ask ourselves, "What is the most important problem business people face today? How will it change tomorrow? What can my company do to solve that problem?

Wayne Gretzky's father told him, "Son, don't look at the puck, look at where the puck is GOING!" Which meant, look to the future.

What are you working on for the future?

"The sun will not be up as soon as I—greet the fair adventure of TOMORROW!"
—Shakespeare

#93 When Faced with a Problem, Ask "What If?"

Don't list the reasons "why not." Throw them out.

Think of the dream. Every business, every building, every country, every invention began with an idea. Think of the ideal solution. Then work out a road map to get from here to there. You can do it.

Thomas Jefferson wrote to his daughter, "Life is like a knife, whirling at you. Grab the handle."

"What if . . ." is progress. "Why not . . ." is failure.

Auguste Rodin's great sculpture "The Thinker" seems to be unfinished. Why? What is his thinking?

#94 When People Tell You "I'll Try"

"OK kids! Ready?!"

Think of a hypnotist who says, "You will try to raise your hand, you will try and try, but you will fail." When the hypnotist wants someone to act, he commands: "Raise your hand, NOW!"

Do not rely on those who say "I'll try." What they are really telling you is, "Chances are, I will not."

"I'll tryers" are not dependable. Release them.

Move on to someone else who says, "Yes! When do you want it done?"

#95 You Are Never Handicapped as Long as You Can Help Someone Else

When Lilly Waters was 11, a forklift tractor fell on her left hand. Her hand was crushed badly, and she was trapped under leakage from the gas tank and received several serious burns. During the first month in the hospital, fighting damage, she lost more than half of her hand. Over the next two years she was operated on eight times to help her regain as much use as possible of what was left of her hand.

One day when Dottie and Bob came to visit her in the hospital, Lilly was asleep because of the painkillers she was given. Dottie became more distressed, so many hopes for Lilly were now dashed. Lilly had just started piano lessons, that dream was over. No typing, no this, no that. So many things required two hands. Almost as soon as they walked in, the little girl in the next bed told them, "You set those bags down and go down the hall to the last room. There is a boy there who thinks he is going to die. His spirit needs to be lifted up." Bob and Dottie marched to the girl's order and did what they could.

As they came back, Dottie was thinking how extraordinary it was for them to have jumped to the command of a child. She asked the girl, "Who are you?"

"I'm Toni Daniels. I go to the handicapped high school here in town."

Dottie said the thought in her mind without thinking, "But you're not handicapped!" The girl radiated power and charisma. Then Dottie looked closer and realized the child was terribly deformed and crippled from polio.

"Well, I've had 32 operations on my spine. But you're right. I'm not handicapped. They teach us at school that you're never handicapped as long as you can help someone else. You might think my friend at school is handicapped. She was born with no arms or legs. She can eat only by rocking back and forth, but she can type with a wand in her teeth. She teaches the typing class. She's not handicapped, either."

"Typing? She can type with no hands?" Hope dawned again. Dottie walked out of the room and phoned IBM. "I understand you have a system for the handicapped to learn to type. My daughter has lost her left hand."

"Lady, no problem. We have charts for people with only a right arm, or left, or no arms! We'll send them right over."

Although Lilly was too young, Bob and Dottie got her into the typing class.

Later that year, Lilly's English teacher scolded Lilly for having someone else do her work. "It's obvious you are not doing this on your own, it's typed!"

"But Sir, I am typing it myself, I learned how."

There was a long silence. "But how? Your left hand . . ."

"Oh, it's a system developed by IBM, I'm up to 50 words a minute with only my right hand," she told him.

"Would they have a way for someone with only a left hand to learn?" The teacher had lost the use of his right arm through polio.

"Sure, the other side of my charts are for people who only use the left hand! Come on, let's go to the typing class now. I'll teach you." Off they went.

That night Lilly told Bob and Dottie, "You know, I'm not handicapped anymore."

#96 Allow People the Gift of Helping You

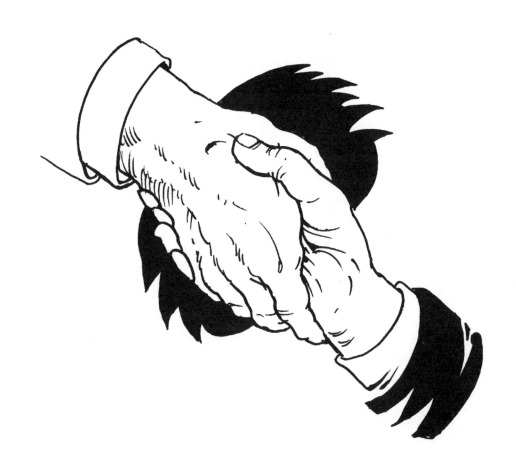

Henri Ruff Dill, of Oregon, was born with no legs. She was determined not to go through life on crutches. As she was learning to use her prostheses, she often fell down. When she went down, she was not able to get up by herself. Instead of filling her with pain and pity for herself, her remarkable mother taught her how very blessed she was. "Dear, when you fall, don't ask just anyone to help you. Look for the person with the saddest face. Reach out to that person. When they help you, smile brightly and say 'Thank you.' Watch how their face will light up with a glow of happiness. The greatest gift you can give is allowing someone to help you. You will make them feel wonderful for days."

#97 Read Biographies—Roadmaps to Success

The library is full of great books—all of them roadmaps, written by the most successful people who ever lived. Ever notice how noisy a bookstore is, with all those voices in the books? The authors are waiting to tell you exactly how they succeeded.

Funny thing, you will be surprised at how often the great stumbled. Their secret is that every one of them got up again.

Read, listen to tapes, watch videos, attend seminars. Catch the bright, valiant spirit of the great achievers, as they got up again and again. Like Bill Marriott of the Marriott hotels, who said:

"Failure? I never encountered it!

All I ever met were temporary setbacks."

#98 True Blue Quality

"Time always tells the truth about things and people who are true blue!"

Do customers like to buy things that are the very best?

Yes, they always have. Quality counts.

One of the most ancient books on earth, written in Arabic, is a recipe book! But it is not for food; it explains how to make dye. In those long ago times, the best blue dye for cloth was made from certain insects. Creating that beautiful deep blue color was a long, hard, laborious process.

Oh, yes, there were fast, slipshod ways to make blue dye. You could buy the cheap dye for much less, but the color faded. It did not last. The quality was not there.

This ancient book told how to test cloth to see if it had been dyed with the best, fine-quality ingredients. The name of the book?

"True Blue." (Yes, that is where those words came from!)

What if you sat down today and asked yourself, "How can I put more quality into every piece of work I put out? How can I make what I do more beautiful, valuable, long-lasting, satisfying, profitable for our customers?"

Give everything you produce the "true blue" test.

#99 From Mr. Einstein—Be a Person of Value

Because we run a large speakers bureau, we have very unusual visitors at our office. We book all kinds of speakers on many subjects.

We love to play "Let's pretend," as many of our audiences do. So our special favorites are the 75 speakers who appear as part of our "Dead Speakers Society." They are characters from history and fiction: Mark Twain, Mae West, Sherlock Holmes, General Patton and many more. Recently, Albert Einstein called on us!

So right here, having a cup of coffee with us at our office, was the man who discovered the world-changing theory of relativity, Albert Einstein (portrayed in costume by Arden Bercovitz).

We asked Mr. Einstein if he had done well in school as a child.

"Oh, no," he replied, "I day dreamed so much they wanted to expel me! Because of the language problem, I had a tendency to think in pictures, not in words."

"Did you think of the theory of relativity as a picture?" we asked.

"Oh yes! As a young boy, I dreamed of riding on a beam of light out into the dark star-spangled sky of the universe. I held a mirror in one hand and a clock in the other. It was that mind-picture that gave me the answer to my theory of relativity."

"What about the problems we face today?" we asked him.

"You see," he twinkled, "a confusion of goals seems to characterize our age. Problems cannot be solved at the same level of consciousness that created them. We must have deep thoughts. Deep pictures. No superficial ones."

Then we asked Mr. Einstein to give us the secret of success. Albert instructed me to tell you this, "The best measure of success . . . ah—to become a *PERSON OF VALUE*."

#100 Lemonade from Lemons

Dottie owned an advertising business that included a one-person office in San Diego in a building she bought through great effort. We had 55 field people, with four managers. Her office lady had a two-week vacation coming, but Dottie couldn't afford a replacement. Dottie decided to run the office herself. She noticed the office was shabby—peeling paint and dead plants.

The team was glum, discouraged, talking about recession. "Our advertisers have no customers!" they told her.

"Ah Ha!" Dottie thought. "If they have no customers, we need to help them find some. *When they succeed, we succeed.*"

Dottie remembered a wonderful quotation from Henry J. Kaiser, the great industrialist. "I always view problems as *opportunities in work clothes.*"

Dottie called her managers. "Come in. We'll help our advertisers get new customers, AND spruce up our office!" Dottie told her staff, "Those who advertise are actively looking for business. They are *waiting* for us!" She scanned the newspaper and phoned painters who advertised there.

Dottie proposed a trade—her advertising service for painting the office. Only five calls and Dottie had a deal. "Let me try for a plant nursery," one of the managers said. "I'm going to help a rug cleaner find customers with our advertising and get this rug shampooed," another said. They all closed those deals.

Dottie said "Well done!" Now let's get some trades going for prizes for our salespeople when they make cash sales. She suggested the type of merchants who would be appropriate. "Call theaters, call restaurants." Within four hours, they had $4,000 in trade prizes. They held a meeting for their salespeople. Everybody was excited when they saw the bright shining office, with paint, plants and prizes.

They added $100,000 in cash billings during those two weeks.

The difference? *Our own attitudes.* As Henry Ford said, "If you think you can, or you think you can't: You are right."

#101 Seize This Precious Moment—"Carpe Diem"

"Unusual . . . yet well-seasoned. I'll take four bags of those home!"

Marcus Aurelius of Rome, who said, "Anything the mind can conceive, and believe, it can achieve," had another slogan *"Carpe Diem!"* (Seize the Day!).

Times were tough, business was slow, when Laura's husband died. She tried to run his gas station herself. Then she got an idea. She knew how to cook the best potato chips anyone ever tasted.

She gave her gasoline customers a free sample, then sold batches of them in brown paper bags. Then she had another great idea. This was a long time ago when things were sold in barrels or drums. Perishable items had a very short shelf life. She invented sealed sacks for her potato chips that would keep them fresh. Laura folded waxed paper and sealed it with her hot iron on her ironing board.

Then Laura went out to call on grocery stores armed with samples for them to taste and her new sacks of potato chips for them to buy. She always wore a hat and a big smile. Her company became one of the largest in the west—*Laura Scudder's.*

A young man in the West told a bartender that the tortilla chips they served were not half as delicious as those his mom cooked at home. The bartender told him to bring in some samples. The bar became a steady customer. You may have heard of the company that developed out of that conversation—*Frito Lay.*

Carpe Diem! Seize the day! Now!

Above
and
Beyond

Dare Mighty Things

"Far better it is to dare mighty things, to win glorious triumphs,
even though checkered by failure,
than to take rank with those poor spirits
who neither enjoy much nor suffer much.
Because they live in the gray twilight
that knows not victory nor defeat."

—Teddy Roosevelt, former President of the United States
(Speech before the Hamilton Club, Chicago, April 10, 1899)

Swing at Every Targeted Opportunity

How many times should we try again when things seem to go wrong? Some folks think that one failure means "time to quit!"

It is what you do when things go wrong that makes the difference. A good example is the great champion baseball player Babe Ruth.

Babe said he looked at the seam on the ball as it was thrown at him. You can't SEE the seam on a ball coming at you at 90 miles an hour!

Babe meant that he focused, concentrated, put his whole life, spirit and intent into his swing—*every time.* Every time the phone rings, put your whole heart into helping the client. Never let your voice say, "You are bothering me, I'm too tired," "We're closed," or "Sorry, that's company policy, there is nothing we can do to help you."

Put your whole heart into your effort on every phone call, every customer contact, every presentation, every piece of work you do.

Some folks concentrate on their failures, instead of on the possibilities.

Babe said something about failure that is very important.

"I never count the misses. I NEVER count the misses—I only count the hits."

Only one man has ever beaten Babe Ruth's record for hits, but NO ONE has ever beaten Babe's record for SWINGS! He tried oftener, and swung harder than anyone else ever has. That is why he was a champion.

How about Mickey Mantle? He came up to bat 8,102 times. He struck out 1,710 times, walked 1,734. Mickey only hit 536 home runs! That means that for 3,444 times at bat, HE NEVER HIT THE BALL. But he put his whole life force into every swing. He was a great champion.

Concentrate on every opportunity. Opportunity is coming your way today. Swing every time! Knock it out of the ballpark for a home run! Remember, "Don't count the misses, just count the hits."

Give It a Rest—
Then Come Back to It

When you have slammed yourself into a challenge so many times you are beginning to turn into the Wicked Witch of the West, stop. Pick up another project you know you can accomplish and enjoy. Maybe let sleep "knit up the raveled sleeve of care."

Then find your "tropopause" time. The Tropopause is the area around the earth where airplanes fly. A band of calm where you can take off your seat belt. The time when your office or house is quiet. You are fresh. Your Tropopause may be in the bathtub, as you jog, in the shower, in your car. During this time your work flies by so quickly that you won't believe the hour is gone. What seemed like a disaster will now be a triumph.

Success Is a Stairway

Many of us feel that we'll struggle and struggle and then—wham! The door will open for us! Sweet success. Not so, life is an unending stairway. Every step can be exciting, joyful, sad, frustrating—whatever you create. The only rule is that there is no stopping on the stairway, and no way off. You go up . . . or. . . .

Surprise Everyone by Giving More than They Expected

You bought the book *101 Simple Things to Grow Your Business*.

Give good measure, compressed and overflowing. Surprise people with more than they expected. They will come back and tell their friends.

Besides, we have an inkling that you will be adding to this list of ideas every day. When you do, we hope you will write, call, fax or E-mail, and tell us about your great system for promoting your business and your career. Remember, there is no limit to what you can accomplish!

"When you close your doors,
and turn out the lights,
Remember never to say that you are alone,
For you are not alone;
God dwells within,
Your Genius dwells within.
And what need have they of light
To see what you can do!

—Dottie's version
(with apologies to Epictetus, from "Discources")

Resources

Sharing Ideas newsmagazine! —For paid speakers, consultants, seminar leaders, meeting planners, bureau owners. Leads, tips, interviews, articles, ideas. Includes book *Speak & Grow Rich,* or book *Secrets of Successful Speakers* or audio album "Everything You've Always Wanted to Know About Speakers Bureaus—But Didn't Know Who to Ask." PLUS: Exclusive International Directory of Speakers Bureaus & Agents—nearly 500 listings in 14 countries

Games Presenters Play. Live seminar by famous speakers Jeff Dewar & Lilly Walters. Get your audience involved, learning, participating. Games, magic, fun ideas and props to get lessons across. How to develop the right game for the right audience. Excellent material.

Teach & Train With Magic. See how to use magic tricks in business presentations. Learn from Magic Castle award-winning Master Magician Tom Ogden. Twelve great tricks to add to your program and put REAL magic in your message.

The Magic of Creativity by Master Magician Tom Ogden. Develop your creativity. Problem solving to make the impossible possible. A magical presentation. Video.

Speaking With Magic. How to grab audience attention and hold it. Use magic in presentations and training sessions. Specific examples. 177 full illustrations, with 32 complete routines by top magician Michael Jeffreys.

Persuasive Platform Presentations: Secrets of Successful Speakers by Lilly Walters. Live seminar includes segments from top professional speakers. Stellar performance tips. Excellent speech training.

Secrets of Successful Speakers, How You Can Motivate, Captivate and Persuade by Lilly Walters. McGraw-Hill Publishers. Major selection by Book-of-the-Month & Fortune book clubs. 63 top world speakers give best secrets on platform skills.

What to Say When You're Dying on the Platform! Complete Resource Book by Lilly Walters. McGraw-Hill. Most comprehensive (easy to use!) survival kit of exactly what to do and say in more than 100 deadly teaching, training/speaking situations. 100 top world presenters advice.

The Greatest Speakers I Ever Heard. Dottie Walters's personal stories. Great speakers she has known and worked with in *Sharing Ideas* newsmagazine and Walters International Speakers Bureau. Intimate, inspiring. Galaxy of speaking stars and pictures.

Never Underestimate the Selling Power of a Woman by Dottie Walters. First book ever written for women in sales. Dynamite techniques, family ideas, creative book.

Selling Power of a Woman. Six hours of sales training by the master herself.

Seven Secrets of Selling to Women. Dottie reveals secrets of persuading women. Learn color and smell; women think differently than men.

Private Career Consultants

Dottie or Lilly Walters available via phone, FAX, or in person. Professional help with materials, titles, marketing, packaging, products. Professional advice. One of Dottie's marketing ideas earned $600,000 for her speaker. Lilly has coached many speakers now in the big leagues, $150 per hour with a two hour minimum. Call to make an appointment.

Speak & Grow Rich
by Dottie & Lilly Walters. The "Bible" of the paid speaking world. Contracts, bureaus, markets, topics and titles. Like a scout manual—how to earn the merit badges. You'll mark it, clip pages, keep it on your desk constantly. The book that has launched thousands of careers. Prentice Hall/Simon Schuster.

Everything You've Always Wanted to Know About Speakers Bureaus—But Didn't Know Who to Ask
by Dottie Walters, President Walters International Speakers Bureau. What bureaus expect from speakers. Do's & don'ts, contracts, catalogs, exclusives, brokering, spin-offs, showcases, client/bureau/speaker relationships. How to have MORE speakers bureaus selling high-fee bookings for you.

How to Enter the World of Paid Speaking.
One of our most popular products. Chosen by *Success* magazine's Chief Editor as "Editors' Choice: Best of the Year." Packed with great ideas. Dottie and Lilly Walters plus a panel of top meeting planners.

How to Build a Lucrative Speaking/Consulting Business.
Dottie Walters with famous Howard Shenson, the "Consultant's Consultant." If you are a consultant now, or want to add consulting profits to speaking, this is great material. Three audio cassettes.

How to Start & Build a Successful Speakers Bureau by Dottie Walters with Somers
White. How to begin a bureau business, what to look out for, how to set fees. Auxiliary income services to sell
to speakers and meeting-planner clients. How to broker celebrities. Bureaus all over the world have thanked us
for this invaluable information. Includes booklet plus a list of speaker-qualifying questions.

How to Create & Market Speaker Products by Dottie Walters & Mike Ferry "King of Back-
Room Sales." Sell thousands of dollars worth of your products at every performance. Why you should create
products, how to do it, packaging, markets, lots more. Includes list of catalogs which carry speaker products.

Anthology Books: Dottie Walters' Royal Publishing creates beautiful Great Speaker Anthologies. Each
speaker writes a chapter. Speaker's picture on front of books they purchase at wholesale. Big profits for retail
sales. Be published quickly. Prestige-publicity. Like to be considered? ☐ Subject? _____

Walters Speakers Services
PO Box 1120
Glendora, Calif., USA, 91740
Phone: 818–335–8069
FAX: 818–335–6127
E-mail addresses via the Internet: LillyW@aol.com or 74117.464@compuserve.com

If you have enjoyed this book you will be pleased to learn that CRISP PUBLICATIONS specializes in creative instructional books for both individual and professional growth.

Call or write for our free catalog:

CRISP PUBLICATIONS, INC.
1200 Hamilton Court
Menlo Park, CA 94025
Tel. (800) 442–7477
FAX (415) 323–5800